from SEA TO SHINING SEA

NORTH CAROLINA

By Dennis Brindell Fradin

CONSULTANTS

Alan D. Watson, Ph.D., Professor of History, UNC-Wilmington

Robert L. Hillerich, Ph.D., Consultant, Pinellas County Schools, Florida; Visiting Professor, University of South Florida

CHILDRENS PRESS®

CHICAGO

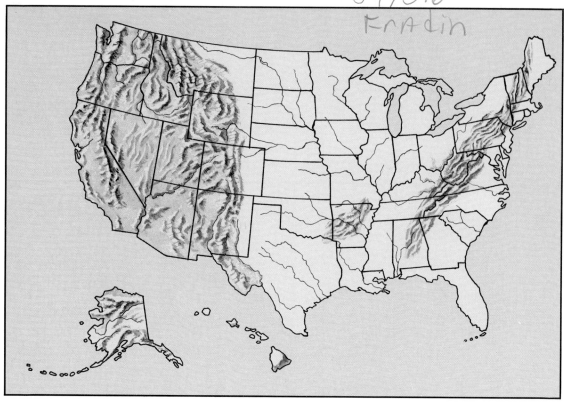

North Carolina is one of the fourteen states in the region called the South. The other southern states are Alabama, Arkansas, Delaware, Florida, Georgia, Kentucky, Louisiana, Maryland, Mississippi, South Carolina, Tennessee, Virginia, and West Virginia.

To Diana Judith Fradin, from Dad, with love

Front cover picture, Bodie Island Lighthouse, Outer Banks; page 1, morning fog in Great Smoky Mountains National Park; back cover, Nantahala River Gorge, Nantahala National Park

Project Editor: Joan Downing
Design Director: Karen Kohn
Research Assistant: Judith Bloom Fradin
Typesetting: Graphic Connections, Inc.
Engraving: Liberty Photoengraving

Library of Congress Cataloging-in-Publication Data

Fradin, Dennis B.
    North Carolina / by Dennis Brindell Fradin.
    p. cm. —(From sea to shining sea)
  Includes index.
  Summary: Introduces the Tar Heel State, its
geography, history, interesting sights, and people.
  ISBN 0-516-03833-8
  1. North Carolina—Juvenile literature. [1. North
Carolina.] I. Title. II. Series: Fradin, Dennis B. From sea to
shining sea.
F254.3.F68 1992
917.5604'43—dc20   91-35576
                                                CIP
                                                 AC

Table of Contents

Gulls at Ocracoke Island

Introducing the Tar Heel State

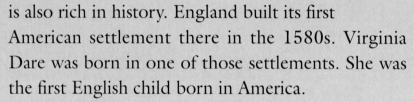

North Carolina is in the southeastern United States. It is a land of lovely woods, mountains, and beaches. The state is also rich in history. England built its first American settlement there in the 1580s. Virginia Dare was born in one of those settlements. She was the first English child born in America.

North Carolina played a big role in the Revolutionary War (1775-1783). Americans fought this war to break free of England and form the United States. North Carolina was the first colony to favor freedom from England.

North Carolina later played a leading role in the Civil War (1861-1865). This war was fought between the northern states and the southern states. North Carolina lost more men than any other southern state. It was said that North Carolina troops stuck to their posts as if held by tar. This may be one reason why North Carolina is called the "Tar Heel State."

*A picture map
of North Carolina*

Today, North Carolina is a manufacturing and farming giant. It is the top state for making textiles (cloth goods) and furniture. It leads the nation in growing tobacco and raising turkeys. The Tar Heel State is special in many other ways. Where did the pirate Blackbeard make his headquarters? Where was the first airplane flight? Where did basketball star Michael Jordan and Presidents James Polk and Andrew Johnson grow up? The answer to these questions is: North Carolina!

Overleaf: Nags Head

5

From the Outer Banks
to the Mountains

FROM THE OUTER BANKS TO THE MOUNTAINS

Norker Carolina is one of fourteen states that make up the region called the South. Four other southern states border North Carolina. Virginia is to the north. South Carolina and Georgia are to the south. Tennessee is to the west. The Atlantic Ocean is to the east.

Off the coast are many islands that are part of North Carolina. Among them are Bodie, Roanoke, Hatteras, and Ocracoke islands. There are also many sandbars and reefs. These offshore parts of North Carolina are called the Outer Banks.

Cape Hatteras, in the Outer Banks, has been called the "Graveyard of the Atlantic" because of all the ships wrecked there.

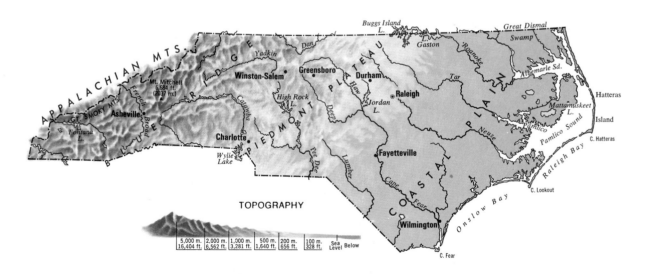

TOPOGRAPHY

| 5,000 m. | 2,000 m. | 1,000 m. | 500 m. | 200 m. | 100 m. | Sea | Below |
| 16,404 ft. | 6,562 ft. | 3,281 ft. | 1,640 ft. | 656 ft. | 328 ft. | Level | |

North Carolina has three land regions. The Coastal Plain takes up the eastern two-thirds of the state. This is North Carolina's flattest, lowest area. The hilly Piedmont region runs through the middle of North Carolina. The state's five largest cities—Charlotte, Raleigh, Greensboro, Winston-Salem, and Durham—are all in the Piedmont. The western fifth of North Carolina is its Mountain Region. The Blue Ridge, Great Smoky, and Black mountains are among the ranges in this area. Mount Mitchell, in the Black Mountains, is the state's tallest peak. In fact, at 6,684 feet, Mount Mitchell is the highest

Cape Hatteras National Seashore (left) is part of the Outer Banks. Hanging Rock State Park (right) is in the northern Piedmont region.

Only about seven other states are as wooded as North Carolina. Wilson Creek (above right) flows through Pisgah National Forest near the Blue Ridge Parkway.

peak in the twenty-six states east of the Mississippi River.

North Carolina is one of our most-wooded states. About two-thirds of the state is forest. Trees found there include pines (the state tree), cypresses, hickories, maples, and oaks.

North Carolina is also a very watery state. Major rivers include the Chowan, the Roanoke, the Tar-Pamlico, the Neuse, the Cape Fear, the Yadkin,

and the Catawba. Lovely waterfalls such as Whitewater Falls can be seen where the rivers tumble over highlands. In the east are some swamps, including Dismal and Green swamps.

Snow falls on the mountains in the wintertime. But, overall, North Carolina's climate is warm. The state does get one dangerous kind of weather. Huge sea storms called hurricanes sometimes strike the coast.

Among North Carolina's lovely waterfalls is Crabtree Falls, in Mitchell County (above left). Wildflowers (above right and opposite page, left) brighten the state.

Overleaf: The Wright brothers' first flight, December 17, 1903

From Ancient Times Until Today

FROM ANCIENT TIMES UNTIL TODAY

Millions of years ago, most of eastern North Carolina was covered by ocean waters. Sharks' teeth and whale bones have been found on what is now dry land. Mammoths and mastodons also lived in North Carolina long ago. Both looked like large, hairy elephants.

Prehistoric Indians reached North Carolina at least twelve thousand years ago. At first, they roamed about hunting bears and deer. Then, they learned to farm.

In later times, about thirty Native American groups lived in North Carolina. The Cherokees lived in the mountains of North Carolina and nearby states. The Catawbas lived along the Catawba River. The Tuscaroras were a big tribe in eastern North Carolina. The Croatoans (or Hatteras) and the Roanokes were small coastal tribes.

Some of those American Indians lived in wigwams. The wigwams were made of wooden poles covered by bark and clay. The Indians grew corn, beans, and squash. They also hunted and fished. Animals and plants provided more than food. Animal skins were

Corn, beans, and squash were so important that the Indians called them the "Three Sisters."

turned into clothes. Small bones made good fishing hooks. Moss was used for babies' diapers.

The Indians held yearly festivals. For example, the Green Corn Dance was held to thank the gods for the summer's first corn. Games and sports were a big part of the festivals. The "ball game" was very popular. Tree poles were sunk into the ground as goalposts. Two teams used sticks to send a deerskin ball toward each other's goal.

The sport of lacrosse developed from the "ball game" played by Indians in Canada.

This village of the Native American Secotans was on the Pamlico River.

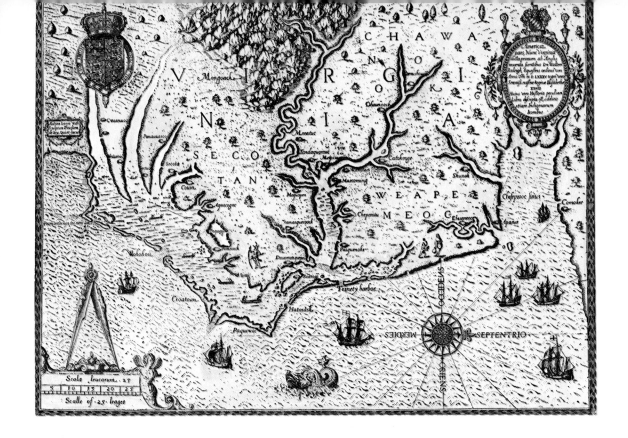

This map of Virginia was made in 1585 by John White and Thomas Hariot. At that time, Virginia included both North Carolina and South Carolina. Many Native American groups known to the Roanoke colonists are shown on the map.

EXPLORERS AND FIRST COLONISTS

In 1492, Christopher Columbus explored some islands not far from Florida. Soon, Europeans were exploring the eastern coast of North America. The first known explorer to reach North Carolina arrived in March 1524. He was Giovanni da Verrazano. Verrazano was an Italian who was sailing for France.

Verrazano loved North Carolina. He wrote about its "sweet flowers" and forests "greater and better than any in Europe." But the French did not settle North Carolina. Spain showed more interest in the region. Spain began colonizing Florida in 1565. The Spanish tried to settle the Carolinas, too. None of their settlements lasted very long, however.

England also hoped to colonize America. In 1584, Englishman Sir Walter Raleigh sent explorers to America. He asked them to pick a good place for a colony. Raleigh's men reported that North Carolina's Roanoke Island was a great spot. The region wasn't called North Carolina then. In early 1585, Queen Elizabeth I gave the name *Virginia* to a large section of land in North America. It included what are now North and South Carolina, Virginia, and several other states.

Raleigh sent six hundred men to Roanoke Island in 1585. They built houses and Fort Raleigh. This was England's first North American settlement. It was called the Ralph Lane Colony (for its governor). The colonists faced many problems. They had to return to England in mid-1586.

Raleigh sent more than one hundred settlers to America in May 1587. John White, an artist, was governor of this group. Among the settlers were White's daughter, Eleanor White Dare, and her husband Ananias Dare.

The settlers reached Roanoke Island in July 1587. They repaired the fort and built new houses.

The Elizabeth II *is a re-creation of the type of ship that brought the first explorers and colonists to North Carolina. The ship is a state historic site.*

On August 18, 1587, Eleanor Dare gave birth to a baby girl. This first English child born in America was named Virginia Dare. A few days later, Governor White sailed to England for supplies. He left instructions. If the settlers left the colony, they were to leave a carving on a tree to tell where they were going.

White was unable to return to America until 1590. When he reached Roanoke Island, he found that all the people were gone. The letters CRO were carved onto a tree near the fort. The whole word—CROATOAN—was carved onto a second tree. White believed that the settlers had gone to live with the friendly Croatoan Indians. Had he gone a few miles

The first English child born in America was christened Virginia because the colony was still called Virginia. It was not yet called North Carolina. Otherwise, she might have been named Carolina Dare.

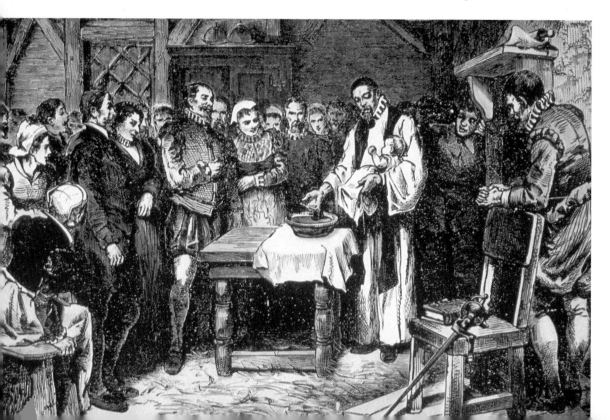

more, he might have found them. But stormy weather and a food shortage forced him to leave.

To this day, we don't know what happened to the colonists. Some people think that they intermarried with the Indians. If so, Virginia Dare's descendants may live in North Carolina today. Other people think that Indians killed the colonists. Because we don't know their fate, Virginia Dare and the others are called the "Lost Colony."

COLONIAL DAYS

In 1607, England built Jamestown, its first permanent American town. Jamestown was in present-day Virginia. That was the first of England's thirteen American colonies. Twenty-two years later, in 1629, King Charles I tried to settle what are now the Carolinas. The king granted a huge piece of Virginia to Sir Robert Heath. Heath was an English official. The land was given the name *Carolana* (Latin meaning "Land of Charles"). However, Heath was unable to settle Carolana.

North Carolina's first settlers came from what is now Virginia. By 1650, good farmland was becoming scarce in the settled areas of Virginia. Some Virginians moved south into the North Carolina

When James White returned to Roanoke Island in 1590, the colonists had disappeared. White found only the word CROATOAN *carved onto a tree.*

19

area to find land. A Virginian named Nathaniel Batts was North Carolina's first known settler. Batts had built a house in northeastern North Carolina by 1655. Other Virginians joined him. By 1660, about a thousand colonists lived in what is now North Carolina.

The region that would become South Carolina still had not been settled. In 1663, the new king, Charles II, changed the name to *Carolina*. That year, he began a new plan of settlement. He granted Carolina to eight lords proprietors (landlords). Settlers could buy or rent Carolina land from the proprietors.

The plan worked. In 1670, settlers sent by the proprietors founded Charleston. It was South Carolina's first town. By 1680, more than five thousand settlers lived in North Carolina. Most of them were poor farmers. For years, North Carolina didn't even have any towns. The settlers lived in the countryside. Bath, the area's first town, wasn't built until 1706.

The Indians grew angry as settlers took their lands. From 1711 to 1713, the Tuscaroras fought the settlers. Several hundred North Carolina settlers were killed during the Tuscarora War. Then, in March 1713, the colonists won a battle near what is

Officially, there was just one Carolina Colony until 1712. But people spoke of North and South Carolina as separate almost from the start.

Bath was named for Bath, England. New Bern, the area's second town, was named for Bern, Switzerland.

now Snow Hill, North Carolina. More than a thousand Tuscaroras were killed or captured. Most of the surviving Tuscaroras left North Carolina.

There was a big change in Carolina during the Tuscarora War. In 1712, it was divided into North Carolina and South Carolina.

Both Carolinas were having problems with pirates. North Carolina's Outer Banks were a favorite pirate hideout. Pirate ships hid around the sandbars and islands. When a ship passed, the pirates raised the Jolly Roger and attacked. The famous pirates Blackbeard and Stede Bonnet robbed ships along the Carolinas' coasts.

The Jolly Roger was the pirates' skull-and-crossbones flag.

In 1718, South Carolina and Virginia sent sailors out to hunt pirates. That year, there were many battles along the North Carolina coast. Stede Bonnet was captured and Blackbeard was killed. After that, piracy was no longer a big threat to the Carolinas.

The proprietors had hoped to become rich from the Carolinas. But that did not happen. In 1729, they sold North Carolina and South Carolina to King George II. Both Carolinas then became royal colonies. The king ruled them through governors.

North Carolina did well as a royal colony. Its people began to do other work besides farming.

Blackbeard's real name may have been Edward Teach.

Salem was begun in 1766. It later grew into the town of Winston-Salem.

The lumber business became important. The "naval stores" business became even bigger. Naval stores were tar and other pine-tree products. They were used to build and repair ships. People poured into the colony. By 1750, its population was seventy-five thousand.

The newcomers began settling in central and western North Carolina. New towns grew. The settlement that became Charlotte was begun about 1750. The settlement that grew into Winston-Salem was founded in 1766.

Frontier families lived differently than coastal people did. By the 1760s, many easterners were well-off or even rich. Black slaves grew tobacco and rice on eastern plantations. Most frontier people

Plantations are very large farms.

22

were too poor to own slaves. They lived in log houses and did their own farming.

There was another difference between the two regions. The easterners ran the government. They gave the westerners little say in it. In 1770, frontier people calling themselves the Regulators rebelled against the government. The Regulators attacked North Carolina's officials. Governor William Tryon sent an army against them. On May 16, 1771, the Regulators lost the Battle of Alamance near Hillsborough. The frontier people did not receive fair treatment until the 1800s.

THE REVOLUTIONARY WAR ERA

Most of the time until the 1760s, England left the thirteen colonies alone. But by 1764, England needed money. To raise funds, England began taxing the Americans. The colonists had to buy tax stamps for such items as newspapers and tea.

Throughout America, men called the Sons of Liberty fought the taxes. Wilmington, North Carolina, was home to many Sons of Liberty. North Carolina women also fought the taxes. In October 1774, women in Edenton, North Carolina, held what is called the "Edenton Tea Party." As a protest

Governor William Tryon faced the North Carolina Regulators in 1771. Tryon was the governor of North Carolina from 1765 to 1771.

The Edenton Tea Party was one of the first acts of rebellion by women in Revolutionary times.

against the taxes, they pledged that they would not use British products. A few months later, the first shots of the Revolutionary War (1775-1783) were fired in Massachusetts. Americans fought it to free themselves from England.

North Carolina's first Revolutionary War battle was an unusual one. It was fought between patriots (Americans who wanted independence) and loyalists (people who remained loyal to Britain). In early 1776, North Carolinian loyalists headed to Wilmington. They hoped to seize the town. North Carolina patriots knew that the loyalists would cross Moores Creek Bridge on the way. The patriots reached the bridge first. They rubbed soap and grease on the bridge. Then, they hid in the woods and waited. About sixteen hundred loyalists reached the bridge on February 27, 1776. As they slid across, the patriots opened fire. About fifty loyalists were killed or wounded. Only one patriot died at the Battle of Moores Creek Bridge.

Six weeks later, North Carolina made a historic decision. On April 12, 1776, it became the first colony to decide to vote for separation from England. That is why "April 12th 1776" appears on the North Carolina flag. Other colonies agreed that independence was best. American leaders in

Philadelphia, Pennsylvania, adopted the Declaration of Independence on July 4, 1776. This paper said that the thirteen colonies were now the United States. William Hooper, Joseph Hewes, and John Penn signed the Declaration for North Carolina.

But America had to win its freedom in battle. About 20,000 North Carolinians fought in many parts of America. A key battle took place in North Carolina: the Battle of Guilford Courthouse. It was fought at what is now Greensboro on March 15, 1781. About 650 British troops were killed or wounded at Guilford Courthouse compared to about 250 Americans. Seven months later, in October 1781, the weakened English army lost the war's last big battle at Yorktown, Virginia. In 1783, the English ended the war and admitted that the United States had won its freedom.

THE TWELFTH STATE

The United States Bill of Rights protects freedom of speech and other basic rights. North Carolina helped bring about the Bill of Rights. In 1787, American leaders created the United States Constitution. Each state would officially join the country when it approved this framework of gov-

Ever since the Declaration of Independence was adopted, July 4th has been celebrated as the birthday of the United States.

The Battle of Guilford Courthouse (above) weakened the British, who soon left North Carolina.

North Carolina's first state house, in New Bern

ernment. One state after another approved. But North Carolina refused without a Bill of Rights. This helped convince United States lawmakers to add a Bill of Rights. North Carolina then approved the Constitution. It became the twelfth state on November 21, 1789. That same year, North Carolina gave up land that seven years later became the state of Tennessee.

For many years, North Carolina's capital had moved around. In 1792, a spot was chosen for a permanent capital. It was in central North Carolina. The town that was built there was named Raleigh for Sir Walter Raleigh. Raleigh has been the state capital since 1794.

In the early 1800s, some North Carolinians did well at growing cotton and tobacco. Yet, the Tar

Heel State trailed the nation in major ways. Its roads were poor. Its towns were small. Manufacturing hadn't grown much since colonial days. Schools were poor and few in number. Because of all this, North Carolina was called the "Rip Van Winkle State." Rip Van Winkle was a fictional man who slept for twenty years.

THE CIVIL WAR

Slavery was North Carolina's worst tragedy. By the mid-1800s, the northern states had ended slavery. But North Carolina and the other southern states still allowed it. Northerners and southerners argued over slavery and other issues for years. Finally, war broke out between the Union (the North) and the Confederacy (the South). This was the Civil War (1861-1865). More Americans were killed in that war than in any other war to this day.

About 125,000 North Carolinians fought for the Confederacy. Confederate General Robert E. Lee said the state's men stuck to their posts as if held by tar. This may be one reason why North Carolina is called the Tar Heel State. About 40,000 North Carolinians died in the war. No other Confederate state lost that many men.

Before the Civil War, most but not all of the black people in North Carolina were slaves. In 1860, the state had about 330,000 black slaves and about 30,000 free black people.

27

More than 2,600 Confederate soldiers were killed or wounded at Bentonville. Union losses stood at 1,600.

The 1862 Battle of New Bern (below) was one of the many Civil War battles fought in North Carolina.

Nearly a hundred Civil War battles were fought in North Carolina. The biggest was the Battle of Bentonville. It was fought on March 19-21, 1865. Three weeks after the Confederates lost this battle, they lost the Civil War. Slavery was ended, and the North and South were kept together in one nation.

Much of North Carolina lay in ruins. Railroads, schools, and homes were wrecked. For a while, during the Reconstruction period, northerners ran the Tar Heel State. Some of them were dishonest men who were out for their own good. North Carolina rejoined the Union on June 25, 1868. Tar Heels then took charge of rebuilding their state.

THE MODERN STATE

The biggest change in North Carolina after the war was the growth of manufacturing. North Carolina had always shipped much of its cotton elsewhere to be made into cloth. Dozens of cotton mills were built in the state in the late 1800s. They made cloth in the Tar Heel State. One of North Carolina's first furniture factories was built at High Point in 1888. By 1900, North Carolina was a leader at making cloth and furniture.

North Carolina was the site of a great event in 1903. That year, Wilbur and Orville Wright of Ohio built an airplane. The Wright brothers brought their airplane to North Carolina. On December 17, 1903, they flew it at Kill Devil Hill on the Outer Banks. This was the first airplane flight in history.

The Wright brothers' first flight took place only about fifteen miles from where the Lost Colony had stood.

Airplanes helped the United States and its allies win World War I (1914-1918) and World War II (1939-1945). Nearly one hundred thousand Tar Heels served in World War I. Nearly four hundred thousand served in World War II. The state produced clothing for United States forces in both wars. Many thousands of American troops were trained at such North Carolina bases as Fort Bragg and Camp Lejeune.

Four black college students conducted the nation's first sit-in at this Greensboro lunch counter.

Meanwhile, tobacco passed cotton as the state's leading crop in the 1920s. By 1930, North Carolina led the nation at making cigarettes, cotton goods, and wooden furniture.

But the state faced big problems such as race relations. Black North Carolinians were treated unfairly. Black adults were stopped from voting. Their children had to attend separate schools from whites. Blacks couldn't even sit with whites in restaurants. All this was true throughout the South even past 1950.

Many North Carolinians fought this injustice. One major event took place in Greensboro on February 1, 1960. That day, four black college students sat down at a lunch counter for whites. They wouldn't leave. Day after day, black people sat at the counter. This began the "sit-in" as a way to fight for black people's rights. After three months, the owners integrated the counter. This meant that both black people and white people could eat there. Many other places in the state were soon integrated. By about 1970, North Carolina's schools had also been integrated.

Meanwhile, industry was growing. In 1959, a research center opened to help industry. It is called the North Carolina Research Triangle Park. Scientists there have made many discoveries, including Astroturf and a medicine to fight AIDS. By 1995, the park had more than fifty research firms.

The research park lies inside the triangle formed by the cities of Raleigh, Durham, and Chapel Hill.

In 1989, both Carolinas suffered a major disaster. That September, Hurricane Hugo struck North and South Carolina. Thanks to early warnings, North Carolina had only two known deaths. But more than two thousand people were injured. Many buildings and millions of trees were destroyed. Rebuilding from Hurricane Hugo has continued well into the 1990s.

North Carolina has been working to improve its schools. In 1985, the state passed the Basic Education Program, which was fully in place in 1995. It provides for smaller classes and other activities which officials hope will help North Carolina's schoolchildren.

Hurricane Hugo destroyed this building in Charlotte.

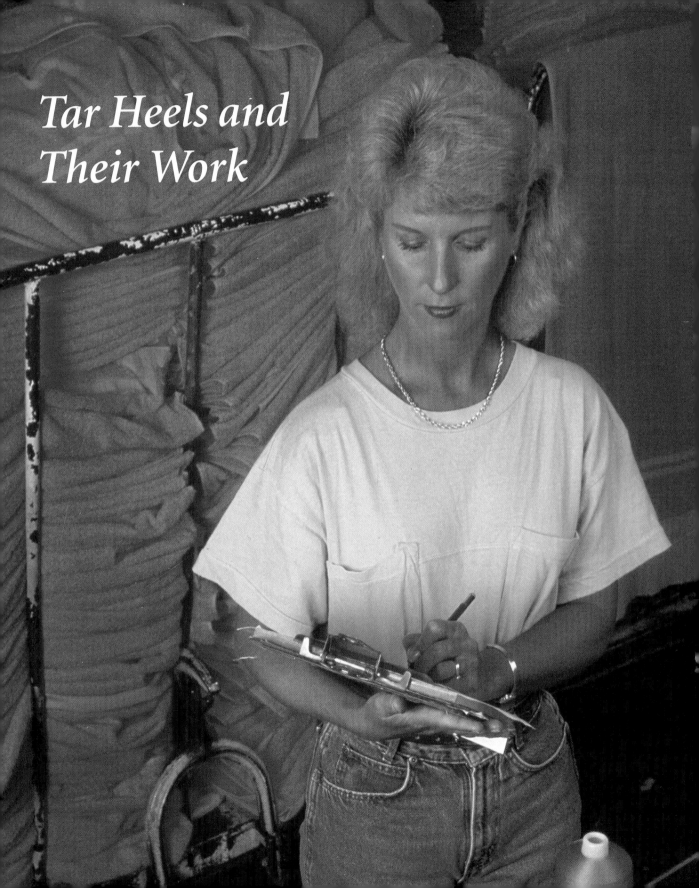

Tar Heels and Their Work

Tar Heels and Their Work

North Carolina has one of the nation's fastest-growing populations. As of 1990, there were about 6.6 million Tar Heels. About 1.5 million North Carolinians are black. About 80,000 are Native Americans.

Making products is the main way North Carolinians earn a living. The state is number one at making furniture and textiles. These include tables, chairs, carpeting, towels, and clothing. The state also leads the nation at making cigarettes. Other major products include medicines, chemicals, machinery, and packaged foods.

North Carolina is a leader in farming. It is the top state for growing tobacco and raising turkeys. Other major farm products include hogs, chickens, soybeans, peanuts, cotton, and apples.

North Carolina is a popular vacationland. Thousands of Tar Heels have jobs in hotels and restaurants. North Carolina is also an important seafood state. Crabs, clams, and shrimp are among the main catches. Sales, banking, government work, construction work, and teaching are also important jobs in the state.

Opposite: A worker at a North Carolina towel factory Overleaf: The Charlotte skyline at night

A commercial fisherman in Manteo

33

A Trip Through
the Tar Heel State

A Trip Through the Tar Heel State

*E*ach year, millions of people visit North Carolina. The Tar Heel State has some of America's most important historic sites. It has interesting cities. The state also has a wide variety of lovely scenery. The Outer Banks would be a good place to start a trip through North Carolina.

The Coastal Plain

The Outer Banks can be reached by car over bridges and by boat. Fort Raleigh, on Roanoke Island, can be thought of as America's birthplace. This was where the English began settling America more than four hundred years ago. Each summer, a play called *The Lost Colony* is performed near the fort. It tells the story of Virginia Dare and the other colonists who disappeared.

The Wright Brothers National Memorial is nearby, at Kill Devil Hill. This was where Wilbur and Orville Wright made the first airplane flight in 1903. That flight went just 120 feet. But it was enough to start the age of the airplane.

The Wright Brothers National Memorial marks the spot where the Wrights made the first powered aircraft flight on December 17, 1903. That first flight lasted just twelve seconds.

The Wright brothers came to the Outer Banks for their strong winds and soft sands. Many kite flyers and hang gliders go there for the same reasons today. The area is also great for swimming, boating, and fishing. Artists like the North Carolina shore. They go there to paint pictures of such landmarks as the Cape Hatteras Lighthouse. At 208 feet high, it is the country's tallest brick lighthouse.

Many people visit the coast to enjoy its wildlife. Geese, ducks, swans, herons, and pelicans are some of the birds that can be spotted. Loggerhead sea turtles weighing hundreds of pounds can be seen. Small numbers of wild ponies live along the Outer Banks. Alligators live in the coastal swamps.

Left: Hang gliding at the Outer Banks
Right: The Cape Hatteras Lighthouse

The wild ponies of the Outer Banks are thought to be descendants of horses brought to North Carolina hundreds of years ago by the Spanish.

North Carolina's oldest towns are along the coast. Bath, its first town, has many buildings from colonial days. Among them is the state's oldest church, St. Thomas, which dates from 1734. Blackbeard lived briefly in Bath. He married a sixteen-year-old girl there. It was said that she was his fourteenth wife.

New Bern, the second-oldest town, is down the coast from Bath. Tryon Palace is in New Bern. It is often called colonial America's prettiest building. Tryon Palace was North Carolina's capitol building at the time of the Revolutionary War.

Wilmington is another historic town along the North Carolina coast. The USS *North Carolina* is docked along the Cape Fear River across from Wilmington. This famous battleship took part in big battles during World War II.

Left: The Tryon Palace gardens, in New Bern
Right: Greenfield Gardens, in Wilmington

The Coastal Plain has rich farmlands. Large amounts of tobacco, corn, and peanuts are grown there. But the region has no very large cities. Fayetteville is the region's biggest city. The Market House is a Fayetteville landmark. It dates from 1838. Slaves were bought and sold in this building.

THE PIEDMONT

The hilly Piedmont region is in the middle of North Carolina. The Piedmont is the state's most-populous area. It is also its center for industry.

Raleigh is at the edge of the Piedmont. In 1994, Raleigh celebrated its two-hundredth birthday as the state capital. Raleigh is also the state's second-largest city.

Raleigh has two main buildings where the government meets. The State Capitol has the governor's office. State senators and representatives meet in the huge State Legislative Building.

Andrew Johnson was born in Raleigh. The house that was his birthplace is in Mordecai Historic Park. Raleigh also has some fine museums. The North Carolina Museum of Art has paintings and sculptures. Some of them date back five thousand years. The North Carolina Museum of History

Inside the State Capitol

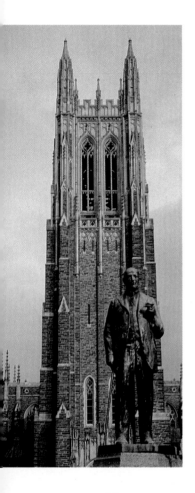

A statue of James Buchanan Duke stands in front of the Duke University Chapel. Duke was born near Durham.

traces the state's history back to ancient times. The North Carolina Museum of Natural Sciences has displays on dinosaurs and other animals.

Durham, the state's fifth-largest city, is northwest of Raleigh. Durham was founded in the 1850s. It was named for Dr. Bartlett Durham, a local landowner. Durham is a cigarette-making center. It is also home to Duke University. This famous school was named for James Buchanan Duke. He was a cigarette maker who gave the school a fortune in the 1920s.

Several old plantations can be seen in the Durham area. One of them is Stagville Center. It has four frame buildings where slaves once lived. They are among the few two-story slave homes still standing in America.

Greensboro is west of Durham. Before the town was built, the Battle of Guilford Courthouse was fought on the site in 1781. General Nathaniel Greene led the Americans at this battle. The town founded there in 1808 was named Greensboro for General Greene. Greensboro is North Carolina's third-biggest city. Clothing, furniture, and cigarettes are made in the Greensboro area. The Greensboro Historical Museum has an exhibit on the famous sit-in of 1960.

Winston-Salem is west of Greensboro. In 1766, a religious group called the Moravians founded Salem. A nearby town called Winston was founded in 1849. In 1913, the two towns combined as Winston-Salem. Today, Winston-Salem is the state's fourth-largest city. Underwear, cigarettes, beer, and food are made there.

Old Salem is a Winston-Salem landmark. The houses and other buildings at Old Salem have been restored. They show what Salem was like in colonial days. The guides at Old Salem dress the way the Moravians did about two hundred years ago.

High Point is a short way from Winston-Salem. High Point is known as the "Furniture Capital of the World." Many furniture makers are in or near

The Moravian Church and the tinsmith shop (above) are among the Old Salem buildings that have been restored. The Moravians originated in what is now the Czech Republic. Winston-Salem is the southern headquarters of the Moravian Church in America.

The Mecklenburg County Courthouse, in Charlotte

the city. High Point is also a leading maker of socks and other hosiery.

Charlotte is southwest of Winston-Salem. The city was settled about 1748. It was named for Queen Charlotte, wife of England's King George III. Charlotte is the largest city in either of the Carolinas. Sheets and towels, banking equipment, and snack foods are made in the Charlotte area.

In 1799, twelve-year-old Conrad Reed found a shiny rock on his farm near Charlotte. The rock weighed seventeen pounds. It was nearly pure gold. Soon, the nation's first gold rush began in the Charlotte area. The Reed Gold Mine is near Charlotte. It was begun by Conrad's family. Visitors to the mine can pan for gold and keep any they find.

From 1837 to 1861, the United States government ran a mint in Charlotte. It used the area's gold to make coins. The building where the mint was located is now the Mint Museum of Art. Gold coins and paintings can be seen there. Discovery Place, a great science museum, is another highlight of the city.

Charlotte is also a sports center. The Hornets, a pro basketball team, play in Charlotte. Near the city is the Charlotte Motor Speedway, where auto races are held.

THE MOUNTAINS

West of Charlotte, the Piedmont hills give way to mountains. The Blue Ridge, Great Smoky, Black, and other ranges are in far western North Carolina. There is a tower on top of Mount Mitchell, in the Black Mountains. People who reach it are as high as anyone can go in the eastern United States.

A road called the Blue Ridge Parkway runs past many scenic spots in the Blue Ridge Mountains. One of them is Grandfather Mountain. It looks like the face of a sleeping old man. Visitors can walk across a mile-high swinging bridge at Grandfather Mountain. Nearby are Linville Caverns. These caves go deep into a mountain. They have strange-looking rock formations. The Blowing Rock is also along the parkway. Winds carry light objects up the

From a distance, their trees give the Blue Ridge Mountains a bluish color.

A view from the Blue Ridge Parkway

side of this cliff. People even joke that snow falls upward at the Blowing Rock.

Asheville is the largest city in the North Carolina mountains. It was laid out in 1794. Asheville was named for Samuel Ashe, a North Carolina governor. Biltmore House is an Asheville landmark. With 250 rooms, it is the country's largest private home. It was built in the 1890s for George W. Vanderbilt. Vanderbilt was a member of one of America's richest families.

Biltmore House, in Asheville

Small farmhouses can also be seen in the mountains. Some of the country people follow the ways of their ancestors. They make their own clothes, quilts, and even furniture. They grow their own vegetables and preserve them for the winter. Parties with square dancing and fiddle music are popular in many small towns.

The town of Cherokee is west of Asheville. The Cherokee Indians have lived in this area for unknown ages. In the 1830s, the United States government ordered the Cherokees to move to Oklahoma. So many Cherokees died on the way that the route was called the Trail of Tears. About a thousand Cherokees hid in the North Carolina mountains to avoid the trip. In 1878, the United States granted the Cherokees land in and around

the town of Cherokee. Today, about eight thousand Cherokees live on and near this reservation. The Oconaluftee Indian Village is in Cherokee. It shows what a Cherokee village was like in long-ago times.

America's most-popular national park is near Cherokee. This is Great Smoky Mountains National Park. The park lies in both North Carolina and Tennessee. Eight million people visit the park each year.

Great Smoky Mountains National Park has beautiful peaks. It has lovely streams and waterfalls. Plenty of wild animals can be seen in the park and elsewhere in the mountains. There are black bears, deer, bobcats, and foxes. Bald eagles, the country's national bird, can also be spotted. Few people have seen a bald eagle in the wild. The eagle population is fairly small. The birds are protected by federal law.

Left: Pioneer cabins in Great Smoky Mountains National Park
Right: A Cherokee man in the Oconaluftee Indian Village. This village was built to look the way a Cherokee village would have looked in the 1700s.

A Gallery of
Famous Tar Heels

A GALLERY OF FAMOUS TAR HEELS

Many famous people have lived in North Carolina. They range from pirates to presidents.

James Knox Polk (1795-1849) was born on a farm near Pineville. Polk was a sickly child. He couldn't do hard farm work. Instead, he was sent off to good schools. Polk graduated from the University of North Carolina. Then he became a lawyer. Later, he entered politics and served as governor of Tennessee. From 1845 to 1849, Polk was the eleventh president of the United States.

Andrew Johnson (1808-1875) was born in Raleigh. He never went to school. Someone taught Johnson to read while he worked in a tailor shop as a teenager. Like James Polk, Johnson went into politics and became governor of Tennessee. In 1864, he was elected vice-president. When President Abraham Lincoln was killed in 1865, Johnson became the seventeenth president. His term was troubled, partly because northerners thought he was too easy on the South after the Civil War.

Andrew Jackson (1767-1845) was the seventh president of the United States. Carolinians have

Johnson was nearly removed from office but served his full term, until 1869.

Opposite: A statue of North Carolina's presidents, James Polk, Andrew Johnson, and Andrew Jackson

Levi Coffin

Dolley Madison

long argued about his birthplace. Jackson was born at the border of the two Carolinas, probably on the South Carolina side. But North Carolina can claim "Old Hickory" anyway, for he studied law there.

Daniel Boone (1734-1820) was born in Pennsylvania. In the early 1750s, Boone and his family made a five-hundred-mile wagon trip to western North Carolina. They lived in a cave during their first winter in North Carolina. After living in North Carolina for many years, Daniel Boone helped to settle Kentucky.

Levi Coffin (1798-1877) was born near New Garden. He hated slavery. As a young man, Coffin opened a Sunday school for slaves. In 1826, he moved to Indiana. He made his home a stop on the Underground Railroad. This was a system by which slaves escaped from the South to Canada. Levi Coffin helped more than three thousand slaves escape.

Dolley Payne Madison (1768-1849) was born near what is now Greensboro. She was one of the nation's most-famous First Ladies. During the War of 1812, the British invaded Washington, D.C. Dolley's husband, President James Madison, fled the White House. Dolley Madison waited until the British were very close before leaving. She took many papers with her. She also took a famous portrait of George Washington. She saved these treasures from falling into British hands.

Braxton Bragg (1817-1876) was born in Warrenton. He became a great soldier. During the Civil War, Bragg was the Confederate commander at major battles.

Hiram Rhoades Revels (1822-1901) was born in Fayetteville. He was a free black person. Revels became a minister. He helped found black churches and schools. During the Civil War, he helped form black units for the Union army. In 1870, Revels was elected to the U.S. Senate from Mississippi. He was the first black U.S. senator.

The Tar Heel State has produced many wonderful writers. **William Sydney Porter** (1862-1910) was born in Greensboro. He quit school when he was about fifteen. Later, he was jailed for taking money from a bank where he had worked. Porter wrote stories under the name O. Henry while in jail. O. Henry became a very famous short-story writer. Novelist **Thomas Wolfe** (1900-1938) was born in Asheville. He wrote *Look Homeward, Angel* and *You Can't Go Home Again*. Children's author **Betsy Byars** was born in Charlotte in 1928. Byars won the 1971 Newbery Medal for *The Summer of the Swans*.

Hiram Revels

Thomas Wolfe

Michael Jordan

Gaylord Perry

North Carolina has also produced many great athletes. Baseball players **Luke Appling, Jim "Catfish" Hunter,** and **Gaylord Perry** were all Tar Heels. Appling (1907-1991) was born in High Point. He won the American League batting title in 1936 and 1943. Perry was born in Williamston in 1938. He won 314 games as a pitcher. Hunter was born in Hertford in 1946. He pitched the Oakland A's and New York Yankees to five championships in the 1970s. Boxing champ **"Sugar Ray" Leonard** was born in Wilmington in 1956. **Michael Jordan** was born in 1963. He grew up in Wilmington. When Jordan was thirteen, his father built a backyard basketball court. Jordan played on it almost every day. He led the University of North Carolina Tar Heels to the NCAA basketball title in 1982. Jordan then became a great pro player with the Chicago Bulls. He helped the Bulls win the 1991, 1992 and 1993 NBA world championships.

Billy Graham was born on a farm near Charlotte in 1918. When he was young, he dreamed of becoming a baseball star. He changed his mind and became a preacher. Reverend Graham has preached to millions of people around the world. He has also written a number of books.

Sugar Ray Leonard's real name is Ray Charles Leonard. His mother named him after the famous singer Ray Charles.

Billy Graham

Roberta Flack

Elizabeth Hanford Dole was born in Salisbury in 1936. She graduated from Duke University. After becoming a lawyer, she entered politics. In 1983, she became the first woman to head the U.S. Department of Transportation. Elizabeth Dole was Secretary of Labor under President George Bush from 1989-1993.

Some famous entertainers have come from the Tar Heel State. The great jazz pianist and composer **Thelonious Monk** (1918-1982) was born in Rocky Mount. Singer **Roberta Flack** was born in the town of Black Mountain in 1940. She won the 1972 Grammy Award for singing "The First Time Ever I Saw Your Face." She won it the next year for "Killing Me Softly with His Song." Actor **Andy**

Elizabeth Dole

Andy Griffith (right) played Sheriff Andy Taylor on "The Andy Griffith Show."

Griffith was born in Mount Airy in 1926. In his earlier years, Griffith played Sir Walter Raleigh in *The Lost Colony.* Later, he became a television star. He played Sheriff Andy Taylor on "The Andy Griffith Show."

Home to Cherokee Indians, Daniel Boone, Dolley Madison, and three presidents . . .

Site of the first English colony in America, the first airplane flight, the highest peak east of the Mississippi, and the country's largest private home . . .

The leader in producing tobacco, textiles, turkeys, and furniture . . .

The first of the thirteen colonies to choose independence from England . . .

This is North Carolina—the Tar Heel State!

Did You Know?

Allie Hill and Maggie Lambeth of Denton were the oldest living twins in the world as of 1989. They were 105 years old.

Boone, North Carolina, was named for Daniel Boone, who had a hunting cabin where the town now stands.

People who don't believe something may call it "bunk" or "bunkum." Long ago, a lawmaker from North Carolina's Buncombe County made a speech that seemed to have no point. People called it "Buncombe." Over the years, this was changed to "bunkum" and "bunk."

When explorers sent by Sir Walter Raleigh reached North Carolina, they asked the Indians what they called the region. The Indians did not understand the question. They said *Wingandacon,* meaning "You wear good clothes." For a few months, the English called what is now North Carolina *Wingandacon.*

Part of the Wright brothers' first airplane is on the moon. Astronauts Neil Armstrong and Buzz Aldrin placed it there when they became the first people on the moon in 1969.

Duke University won the national college basketball championship in 1991 and 1992.

North Carolina has towns named Half Moon, Faith, Mars Hill, Jupiter, Tar Heel, Toast, Cricket, Seven Devils, and Turkey.

North and South Carolina are the only places where the Venus's-flytrap grows in the wild. This unusual plant eats insects. It captures them with its leaves, then gives off a juice that turns them into food.

Every June, the National Hollerin' Contest is held in Spivey's Corner, near Fayetteville. Besides the yelling contest, there is country music, square dancing, and a barbecue.

George Herman Ruth belted his first pro home run in a spring training game in Fayetteville in 1914. It was also in Fayetteville that he was nicknamed "Babe" Ruth.

In 1948, Rocky Marciano tried out for a minor-league baseball team in Fayetteville, but didn't make it. Marciano turned to boxing instead. He became one of the greatest heavyweight champs in history.

Dolley Madison was First Lady for sixteen years—longer than any other woman. President Thomas Jefferson's wife was dead, so Dolley served as his White House hostess for eight years. Dolley was then First Lady for her husband, President James Madison, for another eight years.

NORTH CAROLINA INFORMATION

Cardinal

Flowering dogwood

Area: 52,669 square miles (twenty-eighth among the states in size)

Greatest Distance North to South: About 190 miles

Greatest Distance East to West: About 500 miles

Coastline: About 300 miles

Borders: Virginia to the north; the Atlantic Ocean to the east; South Carolina and Georgia to the south; Tennessee to the west

Highest Point: Mount Mitchell, 6,684 feet above sea level (the highest peak in the twenty-six states east of the Mississippi River)

Lowest Point: Sea level, along the shore of the Atlantic Ocean

Hottest Recorded Temperature: 110° F. (at Fayetteville on August 21, 1983)

Coldest Recorded Temperature: −29° F. (on Mount Mitchell on January 30, 1966)

Statehood: The twelfth state, on November 21, 1789

Origin of Name: North and South Carolina were named in honor of England's King Charles I; the name comes from *Carolana* (Latin meaning "Land of Charles")

Capital: Raleigh (since 1794)

Counties: 100

United States Senators: 2

United States Representatives: 12 (as of 1992)

State Senators: 50

State Representatives: 120

State Song: "The North State," by William Gaston (words) and Mrs. E. E. Randolph (music)

State Motto: *Esse Quam Videri* (Latin meaning "To Be Rather Than to Seem")

Nicknames: "Tar Heel State," "Old North State" (to distinguish North Carolina from South Carolina)

State Seal: Adopted in 1984

State Flag: Adopted in 1885

State Flower: Flowering dogwood

State Bird: Cardinal

State Tree: Pine

State Colors: Red and Blue

State Insect: Honeybee

State Reptile: Turtle

State Mammal: Gray squirrel

State Gemstone: Emerald

Some Rivers: Chowan, Haw, Roanoke, Tar-Pamlico, Neuse, Cape Fear, Yadkin, Catawba, French Broad

Some Islands: Bodie, Roanoke, Hatteras, Ocracoke, Topsail

Some Waterfalls: Bridal Veil Falls, Linville Falls, Whitewater Falls

Wildlife: Deer, black bears, foxes, bobcats, raccoons, beavers, gray squirrels, otters, geese, swans, cardinals, mockingbirds, Carolina wrens, eagles, many other kinds of birds, rattlesnakes and other snakes, alligators, turtles

Fishing Products: Crabs, clams, shrimp, trout, flounder, menhaden, mackerel

Farm Products: Tobacco, turkeys, chickens, hogs, corn, soybeans, peanuts, cotton, apples and other fruits, sweet potatoes, cucumbers

Mining: Limestone, feldspar, granite, marble, sand and gravel, clay

Manufacturing Products: North Carolina is first in the nation in producing furniture, textiles, and tobacco products; other products include medicine, chemicals, machinery, packaged foods, computers

Population: 6, 628, 637, tenth among the states (1990 U.S. Census Bureau figures)

Major Cities (1990 Census):

Charlotte	395, 934	Durham	136, 611
Raleigh	207, 951	Fayetteville	75, 695
Greensboro	183, 521	High Point	69, 496
Winston-Salem	143, 485		

Honeybee

Gray squirrel

Turtle

NORTH CAROLINA HISTORY

Explorers sent to Roanoke Island by Sir Walter Raleigh traded with the Native Americans.

About 10,000 B.C.—Prehistoric Indians live in North Carolina

1524—Giovanni da Verrazano explores North Carolina's coast

1526—Spain tries but fails to settle the Carolina coast

1584—English explorers sent by Sir Walter Raleigh visit Roanoke Island

1585—Englishmen sent by Raleigh build England's first North American settlement on Roanoke Island; it is soon abandoned

1587—The second colony is established under John White on Roanoke Island; Virginia Dare is born there

1590—White returns to Roanoke Island; the colony has disappeared

1629—King Charles I gives a huge piece of Virginia to Sir Robert Heath, who names it *Carolana*, for the king

1663—Charles II changes the name to *Carolina* and grants it to eight lords proprietors (landlords)

1706—North Carolina's first town—Bath—is founded

1711-13—Indians are defeated in the Tuscarora War

1712—North and South Carolina are made separate colonies

1729—North Carolina becomes a royal colony

1751—James Davis founds the colony's first newspaper, the *North Carolina Gazette*, at New Bern

1775—The Revolutionary War begins; Mecklenburg County patriots reportedly issue the Mecklenburg Declaration of Independence

1776—Patriots win the Battle of Moores Creek Bridge; North Carolina becomes the first colony to decide to vote for independence

1781—The English suffer heavy losses in the Battle of Guilford Courthouse

1783—The Americans win the Revolutionary War

1789—North Carolina becomes the twelfth state

1794—Raleigh becomes the capital

1795—The University of North Carolina is the first state university to open; James Polk is born near Pineville

1808—Andrew Johnson is born in Raleigh

1845—James Polk becomes the eleventh president of the United States

1850—The population of North Carolina is nearly one million

1861—The Civil War begins

1865—The Confederates lose the Battle of Bentonville; the war ends; Andrew Johnson becomes the seventeenth president of the United States

1901—Charles B. Aycock, the "Education Governor," begins a program to improve the public schools

1903—Wilbur and Orville Wright make the first airplane flight

1917-18—After the United States enters World War I, nearly 100,000 Tar Heels serve

1930—By this year, North Carolina leads the nation in making wooden furniture, cotton goods, and tobacco products

1941-45—After the United States enters World War II, nearly 400,000 Tar Heels serve

1960—"Sit-ins" are begun at Greensboro

1971—The new state constitution takes effect

1985—The 400th anniversary of the founding of the first English colony in America, on Roanoke Island; North Carolina passes its Basic Education Program

1989—Hurricane Hugo kills at least two people and causes $1 billion in damage in North Carolina

1993—Hurricane Emily causes $10 million in damage

The University of North Carolina at Chapel Hill opened in 1795.

By 1930, North Carolina led the nation in making wooden furniture.

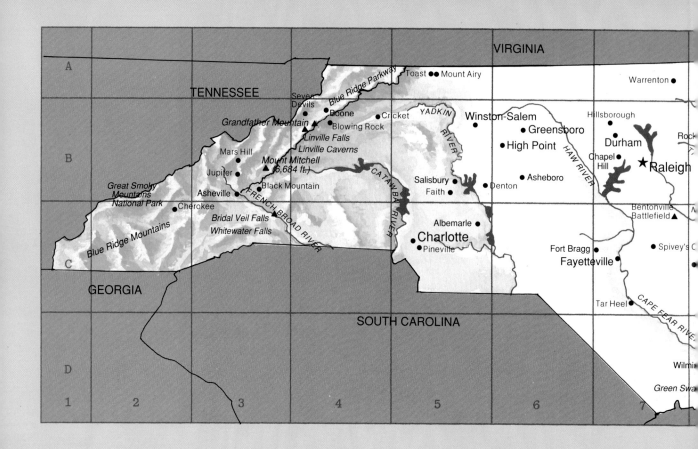

MAP KEY

Albemarle	C5	Dismal Swamp	A9	Mount Airy	A5		
Asheboro	B6	Durham	B7	Neuse River	C8		
Asheville	B3	Faith	B5	New Bern	C9		
Atlantic Ocean	D9,10	Fayetteville	C7	Ocracoke Island	C10		
Bath	B9	Fort Raleigh	B10	Pamlico River	B8,9		
Bentonville Battlefield	C7	Fort Bragg	C7	Pineville	C5		
Blowing Rock	B4	French Broad River	B,C3,4	Raleigh	B7		
Blue Ridge Parkway	A,B4	Grandfather Mountain	B4	Roanoke Island	B10		
Blue Ridge Mountains	C2	Great Smoky Mountains		Roanoke River	A,B8,9		
Bodie Island	B10	National Park	B,C2	Rocky Mount	B8		
Boone	B4	Green Swamp	C7,8	Salisbury	B5		
Bridal Veil Falls	C3	Greensboro	B6	Seven Devils	B4		
Camp Lejeune	C8	Half Moon	C9	Spivey's Corner	C7		
Cape Fear River	C,D7,8	Hatteras Island	C10	Tar Heel	C7		
Catawba River	B,C4,5	Haw River	B6	Tar River	B8		
Chapel Hill	B7	Hertford	A,B9	Toast	A5		
Charlotte	C5	High Point	B6	Topsail Island	D8		
Cherokee	C2	Hillsborough	B7	Turkey	C8		
Cricket	B4	Jupiter	B3	Warrenton	A7		
Denton	B5	Kill Devil Hill	B10	Whitewater Falls	C3		
		Linville Falls	B4	Williamston	B9		
		Linville Caverns	B4	Wilmington	D8		
		Mars Hill	B3	Winston-Salem	B5		
		Mount Mitchell	B3	Yadkin River	B5		

60

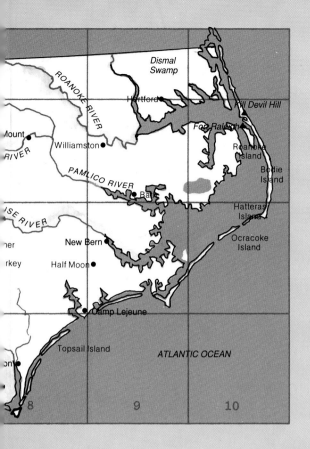

GLOSSARY

ancestor: A person from whom one is descended, such as a grandfather or a great-grandmother

ancient: Relating to those living at a time early in history

Bill of Rights (of the United States): Laws that protect freedom of speech and other basic rights of Americans

capital: The city that is the seat of government

capitol: The building in which the government meets

coast: The land along a large body of water

colonize: To found a colony

colony: A settlement outside a parent country and ruled by the parent country

Confederacy: A short name for the Confederate States of America, the country the South formed at the start of the Civil War

construction: The process of building homes and other structures

descendants: People who are related to people of an earlier time

explorers: Those who travel in unknown lands to seek information

factory: A place where things are made

frontier: A place that has just started to become developed

hurricanes: Huge storms that form over oceans

independence: Freedom

million: A thousand thousand (1,000,000)

patriots: Persons who love and support their country

pirates: Robbers who operate on the high seas

population: The number of people in a place

prehistoric: Before written history

research: Careful study by scientists or other experts

scarce: Not plentiful; rare; hard to get

settlers: People who move to an uninhabited area

slavery: A practice in which people are owned by other people

PICTURE ACKNOWLEDGMENTS

Front cover, ©Lani/Photri; 1, © J. Patton/**H. Armstrong Roberts**; 2, **Tom Dunnington**; 3, © Barbara L. Moore/**N E Stock Photo**; 4-5, **Tom Dunnington**; 6-7, © Barbara L. Moore/**N E Stock Photo**; 8, **Courtesy of Hammond, Incorporated, Maplewood, New Jersey**; 9 (both pictures), © **Tom Till/Photographer**; 10 (left), © Skip Moody/**M.L. Dembinsky, Jr.**; 10 (right), © **SuperStock**; 11 (left), © **H. Armstrong Roberts**; 11 (right), © **Buddy Mays**; 12-13, **Library of Congress**; 15, **North Wind Picture Archives**; 16, **North Wind Picture Archives**; 17 (both pictures), © **Ernest H. Robl**; 18, **Historical Pictures Service, Chicago**; 19, **North Wind Picture Archives**; 21, **North Wind Picture Archives**; 22, **Wachovia Historical Society, Winston-Salem, N.C.**; 23, **North Wind Picture Archives**; 25, **North Wind Picture Archives**; 26, **North Carolina Division of Archives and History**; 27 (top), **Courtesy of the New York Historical Society, New York City**; 27 (bottom), **Penn School Papers, Southern Historical Collection, University of North Carolina at Chapel Hills**; 28, **North Wind Picture Archives**; 30, **UPI/Bettmann**; 31, **Wide World Photos, Inc.**; 32, © Chip Henderson/**Tony Stone Worldwide/Chicago Ltd.**; 33, © Bill Howe/**Photri**; 34-35, © Gerald Fritz/**Tony Stone Worldwide/Chicago Ltd.**; 36, © Dave Brown/**Journalism Services**; 37 (left), © Barbara L. Moore/**N E Stock Photo**; 37 (right), © Don Smetzer/**Tony Stone Worldwide/Chicago Ltd.**; 38 (left), © Bob Glander/**SuperStock**; 38 (right), © **SuperStock**; 39, © Sheryl S. McNee/**Tony Stone Worldwide/Chicago Ltd.**; 40, © **Joseph A. DiChello, Jr.**; 41 (left), © **SuperStock**; 41 (right), © Robert Perron/**Tony Stone Worldwide/Chicago Ltd.**; 42, © Steve Murray/**Picturesque**; 43, © Bryan Allen/**SuperStock**; 44, © **Arch McLean**; 45 (left), © Tom Algire/**SuperStock**; 45 (right), © **Virginia R. Grimes**; 46, © Murray & Associates/**Tony Stone Worldwide/Chicago Ltd.**; 48 (top), **Dictionary of American Portraits**; 48 (bottom), **Historical Pictures Service, Chicago**; 49 (top), **North Wind Picture Archives**; 49 (bottom), **AP/Wide World Photos**; 50 (top), © Charles Gupton/**Tony Stone Worldwide/Chicago Ltd.**; 50 (bottom), **AP/Wide World Photos**; 51 (both pictures), **AP/Wide World Photos**; 52 (both pictures), **AP/Wide World Photos**; 53, **AP/Wide World Photos**; 54 (left), **AP/Wide World Photos**; 54 (right), **Duke Sports Information photo**; 55 (left), © Kerry T. Givens/**Tom Stack & Associates**; 55 (right), **North Carolina Travel & Tourism Division**; 56 (top), **courtesy Flag Research Center, Winchester, Massachusetts 01890**; 56 (middle), © Richard Piliero/**N E Stock Photo**; 56 (bottom), © Roger Bickel/**N E Stock Photo**; 57 (top), © John Kohout/**Root Resources**; 57 (middle), © Tom Hannon/**N E Stock Photo**; 57 (bottom), © James P. Rowan/**Marilyn Gartman Agency**; 58, **Historical Pictures Service, Chicago**; 59 (top), © Billy E. Barnes/**Tony Stone Worldwide/Chicago Ltd.**; 59 (bottom), © **Cameramann International, Ltd.**; 60-61, **Tom Dunnington**; back cover, © **Larry Ulrich Photography**

INDEX

Page numbers in boldface type indicate illustrations.

63

ABOUT THE AUTHOR

Dennis Brindell Fradin is the author of more than one hundred published children's books. His works for Childrens Press include the Young People's Stories of Our States series, the Disaster! series, and the Thirteen Colonies series. His other books are *Remarkable Children* (Little, Brown) and *How I Saved the World* (Dillon). Dennis is married to Judith Bloom Fradin, a high-school English teacher. They have two sons, Tony and Mike, and a daughter, Diana. Dennis graduated from Northwestern University in 1967 with a B.A. in creative writing, and has lived in Evanston, Illinois, since that year.